Night Writing

Kathryn Lomer grew up in north-west Tasmania and lives in Hobart. She has published across the genres of novel, short story, young adult fiction and poetry. Her books have received a number of awards, including a NSW Premier's Literary Award, the Anne Elder Award and the Margaret Scott Prize.

Kathryn Lomer
Night Writing

UQP

First published 2014 by University of Queensland Press
PO Box 6042, St Lucia, Queensland 4067 Australia

www.uqp.com.au
uqp@uqp.uq.edu.au

Cover design/illustration by Sandy Cull, gogoGingko
Author photograph by Esther Ottaway
Typeset in 11.5/14 Adobe Garamond by Post Pre-press Group, Brisbane
Printed in Australia by McPherson's Printing Group

National Library of Australia cataloguing-in-publication data is available at:
http://catalogue.nla.gov.au

ISBN 978 0 7022 5003 3 (pbk)
ISBN 978 0 7022 5234 1 (epdf)
ISBN 978 0 7022 5235 8 (ePub)
ISBN 978 0 7022 5236 5 (Kindle)

University of Queensland Press uses papers that are natural, renewable and
recyclable products made from wood grown in sustainable forests. The logging
and manufacturing processes conform to the environmental regulations of the
country of origin.

For Laura,
with admiration and love

Contents

The mother hand

Rainbow angle

Holy days

The mother hand

Gilded

My palomino reached fourteen and a half hands
when I turned fourteen and a half.
Then came the breaking-in,
ribs too narrow for comfort, stride skittish,
coltish.

Boys came to ride with me,
half-known boys,
their names like ripe berries,
and long hair tied in ponytails.
We tracked over spitting summer paddocks,
crackly, combustible,
horses sweating under us,
swatting flies with sharp tail-thwacks.

We galloped;
fear of the tilting earth thrilled us.
Always an element of danger:
the bolt, the buck, the roll.
We rode boundaries,
occasionally crossing,
leaving fencelines behind for bush,
pretending to adventure.
Sometimes we rode to the pine forest,
where needles lay like a mattress on forest floor
and hushed everything.
Sometimes, resting, we fished for yabbies.

When the boys had gone
my mother and I washed my horse
with the carwash brush and a hose,
my mother in slacks,
my face half-hidden behind loose long hair.
I would learn this act had the intimacy
of knowing a man's body,
skin rippling under touch.

My hands were all over him:
I picked up his hooves gently,
hooking out the sour scent
from a tender frog,
amazed at the soft secrets within horny feet.
Curry comb, brush, hay and oats:
this is how I learned to care for another,
the looking-after love requires.
Nicknamed Shandy for his colour,
he had a smart breed name –Tshinta,
something exotic, an otherness I desired.
I would whisper the foreign syllables
into his twitching ear,
nuzzle the velvet lips,
cry into his unkempt mane for want of friends.
I pictured him wild on a faraway plain
galloping with his mob
like the stallion in *Wildfire*.

In winter he paled and grew shaggy.
Summer gilded him; he glowed,
a muscled sun.

The vet came and cut out his testicles.
I remember the hard bite
on the moon of my backside
next time I picked up his hoof.
The bruise flowered on my young skin
for seven weeks.

The mother hand
(*On dipping into the new Auslan dictionary*)

THE OKAY HAND
I find the sign for a close friendship,
especially one involving romantic
or sexual feelings. This is more like it.
I mean, *relationship*!
any romance lost in translation.
You're okay; I'm okay:
put us together.
I believe it when you say
everything is going to be all right.

THE POINT HAND
Next I learn *sweetheart*.
I try it out in rooms full of people,
half hoping there's someone who reads me
or that it rises from chest to larynx
of its own accord, outed.
Looking down, I find the shape
imprinted on my T-shirt.
I'm planning to teach it to you, pointing:
here, have a heart.

THE HOOK HAND
Ache, of all kinds,
its shape unforgettable, already known,
as if I've been trying to hook

or hold on to something forever.
Even something small;
god is in the small things.
For these I'd need the Soon Hand:
worn like an epaulette
it means *trust*.

THE TWO HAND
Our teacher tells us the Deaf can be blunt,
difficult truths always told, and no social niceties.
Perhaps it's harder to lie with your hands,
changing one lexeme in a sleight.
Anyway, lies show up all over the face;
you can always spot them given practice,
and the Deaf are expert observers.
Still, here is the sign, made from double talk,
one variant followed by *crying*.

THE WISH HAND
An eloquent hand in anyone's language.
Fingers crossed like children's
in a two-handed sign,
the same for *wish* and for *hope*.
Perhaps nothing is impossible
and children know it.
Saying *sorry* requires both hands, too,
wound like ribbon and tied in a bow.
And change.

The Mother Hand

This hand is used very little:
Mum! Mum!
Minute and *month* are the same;
put them together
for the woman who gave birth.
Minutes for conception, months pregnant.
Mothers know time, from then on, is elastic.
There's also, oddly, *maiden*,
but that's cricket.

The Flat Hand

I love you comes right below *butterfly*,
hands like wings over the heart
ready to flap away, or alight.
At the chest, hands push a baby upwards,
from womb to world, an offering: *birth*.
Next page, *burial*: on edge now, hands place a body into earth,
again from the chest, as if burying their heart.
My friend says, *Don't worry so much about life:
it's not permanent.*

The Bad Hand

A shock to find *son*; only here
because spelled out with a little finger.
I could use the Spread Hand sign
for sunrise, lighting my life.
Now we learn Auslan together

and practise when playing cards.
It is gentler than this year's language.
We say nice things to each other:
Your turn. Good luck. Go fish.

THE AMBIVALENT HAND

Combining good and bad,
this is the hand life tends to deal:
anything that can happen, will happen.
Our downfall is to expect otherwise.
It seems in any language
there's some grand design for heartbreak,
words ripe for all occasions.
We use this hand to say,
I *judge*.

THE LOVE HAND

Placed arbitrarily at the back; one page.
Besides a shorthand *I love you*,
it signals *bad temper*, *bad luck* and *bad taste*.
Imagine turning on the bedside lamp
in order to say I love you.
Or not even bothering,
having learned through experience
trust in the body
to say everything.

The lion

The day the lion escapes,
zoo-keepers are frenzied:
liability insurance could go through the roof.
The last lion to escape, from Taronga,

shredded a wedding party in the gardens next door.
Guests ran for cover
before the knot could be tied.
I have it that the lion ran off with the bride,

neither seen again;
that's been my trouble –
wishing the impossible,
lacking the courage for reality.

The lion symbolises courage;
Saul Bellow's Henderson sought it in Africa
in the skin of a lion.
As a new mother I took on a totem,

a creature whose traits I admired.
I chose *leopard*: beauty, strength for the fight,
speed for flight, but I might exchange my spots
for courage, though it does the lion no good

when they decide to shoot her.
I once read that love is mainly courage.
It makes me think of Anna Politkovskaya
who loved truth,

even the hard truths of Chechnya and North Caucasus.
Born in 1958, like me,
she got all the courage there was that year.
They shot her, too.

Compass

The boy's sandpit has transformed
into a vegetable plot:
the edible backyard.

Like everything in their home,
it is chaotic.
Radishes and beans have gone to seed
while cherry tomatoes gleam red
in unexpected places.
The boy eats them straight from the vine;
there is not a single thing that's formal.
Silverbeet shines,
the green of a racing car.

Sunflowers have a slow start;
their darling faces still crumpled
like a baby's, instead of all smiles,
the sun having shifted too low in the sky;
they don't know where to look.

This is one way to say it:
the woman had a child
and everything changed.

She heard about a boy who,
asked to donate rare blood for his brother,
thought for an hour, then agreed,
only later asking
when he would begin to die.

Nothing she knows of sacrifice
comes near.

Still there were times the woman's ego
was no bigger than the paring
she cut from her son's little toenail.

Cleaning, she finds her dead father's barometer –
the shape of a ship's wheel –
stashed in a drawer,
remembers its fate:
knocked to the floor by the child.
The child cried as the pegs of the wheel snapped
and its glass cracked.
One hand will always point to Fair,
one to Change.

She uses others' poems to chart her life;
only the child has a compass,
but the stars are always there,
constant, changing.

It's a small plot;
pumpkins jump their boundary boards
and creep about. They grow
when no one's looking.
It's like a game of statues,
says the boy. Who moved?

She remains uncertain.
Her talisman:
the sky's ever-changing clouds.

Clouds are always made of the same stuff.
They look white
because the light's refracted.
It's always about light.

The light on her son's cheek.
He's like a spring leaf,
unfurling.

Dear life

A scarlet robin in a red vest,
    and his plain love,
        mate above our heads,   out on a limb.
    It *is* spring, you say.
          New Holland honeyeaters flirt
with the light
    and the sight of each other.
        Green rosellas blend into snow gums
then a piece of tree
          takes flight beside us.

    Eucalypt forest below is struck through with white stags,
          dead trunks reflecting the sun.
I'm thankful winter's done,
         that warmth seeks us out
and lures the growth of branch, blossom, leaf.

The Organ Pipes' sudden soar of sheer dolerite
         outshines cathedrals,
    vaulting above us,
  clouds racing past the precipice;
    it falls towards us,
          or we fall towards the sky.
    In crevices and cracks
plants hang on for dear life,
    thrive, even, in their stronghold.

Beneath me,
    three hundred and fifty metres of rock
thrust through the old crust
              of limestone,
Jurassic through Triassic,
     and lower,
         Permian.
Fossils we've found at the end of your foothill street
    reveal creatures we'd find on a beach.

    Voices of climbers reach us on the thin air,
ribbons of sound fluting
       through the stone amphitheatre.
    We trace demarcations of botanical change –
       the last snow gum,
a new community of alpine scrub –
    due to temperature, wind, rain shadow.
Microclimates patchwork vegetation.

    Hakea nuts lie among stones
like hearts cracked open,
     emptiness at their centre;
       or a seed like the gauzy wing of an insect
cleaves to the side,
    a filament of hope.

When a mountain skink and I
      size each other up,
  his lungs pump a mottled flank.
        I envy his reptilian coat,
    the colour of lichen
        and rock.

Layers of city glaze craze and fall away;
my skin glows green.
       I am coming undone.

      Spoor of creatures
which inhabit the night
         and know this place not by sight,
or by heart like you,
    but by touch, and smell, and sound;
the ground they tread threads a wild pattern
      across scree slopes,
among alpine plants,
        tracing vagaries of hunger and fear.
I know it's tooth and claw
   but up here
everything appears to have its place.

     We clamber over boulders
         strewn like marbles,
rolled and eroded
    by the thumb of millennia.
Frost-cracking and loss continue,
    the washing away;
      polygonal columns sway
and fall unseen.
      When you climb the boulder
on which I lean
       I feel it tremble,
like my body under your warmth.
    Hundreds of millions of years to become this,
and still ravelling
      beneath our scrambling hands.

Up through the rock chimney in the north buttress
        your ascent is laid-back.
                I stall and stumble,
the swoop in my stomach
            like that of earth tremors felt in the night.
You ask if I'm afraid. *Yes.*
        But then I'm in the mountain's rock embrace,
and through.

Nooks and crannies of curlicued coast
        now unfurl. Below us, clouds fray
                and race shadows
over green peninsulas
                and Channel blue.
For once, I know exactly
        where I stand.

Bedlam Walls

Hush the wind in rigging
and we might hear voices locked in stone.

This was a bay of fires:
tribes gathered on the promontory
to bask in winter sunshine like today's.
Its coast is discordant,
cut with bays and rock shelves,
a place where shellfish thrived,
the shortest river crossing in a rolled-bark canoe.

Middens have been mined for lime and shellgrit;
still the white is bright throughout the earth.
Cave stone is soft, eroded;
we place our hands inside the empty sphere
where once a harder rock cleaved
like a cannon ball in the cliff face.

Looking out from the cave mouth,
I ask my son why there are waves today.
A giant octopus, he says,
is wriggling his tentacles.
It might be a fire story once told here
with age-old innocence,
before the massacre.

The race fleet goes about with the wind;
mainsails flap and billow
like handkerchiefs raised in urgent surrender.
Then: silence.

The passion

I.

Our church was built by its congregation on weekends –
yes, on Sundays – from weatherboard and corrugated iron.
It was where a small town worshipped.
I liked that word, *worship*,
and all the kissing that went with it –
garments, feet, the ground on which Jesus trod –
plotting, even back then, a passionate life.
I knew the plaster saints like friends,
studied them while Latin droned to its end.
I thought they all wore holy robes, like clergy.
One year, our Archbishop paid a visit.
Your worship, I said slowly, kissing his gold ring.
At confession, I made up sins,
beginning a lasting passion for fiction.
Some sins I didn't even understand
but the nuns told them to us as examples.
At Mass, I'd sing with the choir up the back
where Sister Patricia pumped the old organ,
and often I did the bible reading,
stories with settings that didn't convince.
In my spare time I'd make the Stations of the Cross,
for bonus points in grace.
Grace was a good word, too,
something I lacked as I grew older.
I made an altar in my bedroom, but who to worship?

II.

Having rested in the Gardens of Gethsemane,
in the shade of an ancient olive tree,
watching sunlight play in a mysterious way
among its leaves, I set off for the Via Doloroso.
In through the walls of Jerusalem,
till then a place name in the highlands,
where people also make pilgrimage,
the way they do to this Wailing Wall.
I never saw so many guns in one place.
I trace Jesus' hallowed footsteps,
follow his passion, but find a boy to kiss
instead of this street of sorrows.
It's the last time I'll ever make the Stations of the Cross.
I prefer to see what's shaking
in the *suq*, play *shesh besh* with the Arabs
in the Market of the Inn of Olive Oil,
smoke their hubbly-bubbly pipes.
The Church of the Holy Sepulchre is a tomb;
I choose life. I don't get to Bethlehem for Christmas:
security's too tight. But I visit Nazareth,
the Sea of Galilee, the Jordan River.
It's a story: one man's life and suffering among many.
Every person has their cross to bear, the nuns used to say
as they fiddled with their waistband crucifix.
One said my mother had *me*.

III.

The old Irish Catholic cemetery
is full of children's graves.
The painter notices more names begin with C

than any other; M is a close second:
all those Mc's and Murphys.
He photographs the colours
of lichen and weathered stone.
If god is in the details,
he has a lot of god to take home.
Some headstones lean, or lie askew,
worn bare of all lettering.
You're a long time dead, I keep hearing.
The western sky turns biblical,
its stratocumulus gilt-edged,
rays of light fanning across the Shoalhaven valley.
Our common Catholic childhoods revive:
Dutch and Irish, much the same.
Those rays, he says, *are really parallel.*
He's a painter, he knows about perspective,
and the way he looks at light is more respectful.
I've learned from that.
Light gives us life: this is the miracle.
I know these rays are a scattering of light
by water droplets and other particles;
they're called *crepuscular*:
god is in the words.

Event horizon

A girl is crying on the Cleveland train.
She's also eating chocolate; it doesn't help.
A man in an Akubra with a stock-whip hatband,

and wearing R.M. Williams boots, watches, rapt,
as her tears fall and spread on denim,
like the first drops of rain on dry earth.

When she alights, he frowns at his quiet wife;
there's something he hasn't understood.
The city stretches itself like a big cat,

roars under its breath, and won't stop.
Sunshine strays through bare jacarandas.
I spend all afternoon at the state gallery, waiting,

considering the painted prayers of Ian Fairweather,
how he barely balanced this tightrope act of living.
A Japanese tourist teeters by on stiletto-heeled, beaded thongs.

A wild duck swims among sculptures in the gallery pond;
fountains soothe her city-ruffled feathers, and mine.
When you arrive to hug me by the mirror pool,

I could forget why you're here.
Doctors have probed, questioned, measured;
they don't appreciate your jokes.

You read their faces like a news bulletin.
We sit by the Buddhist temple and talk of the future.
Planes pass over, land, and leave

with their fragile cargo of flesh and faith,
people afraid, flying anyway.
I'm through with being scared,

pared down like soapstone to a too-smooth shape.
There is no reason why this day will work,
but days are all we have.

Mornings are best; the light wakes us with crows,
with trains, and lines that break from the heart.
We rise amid the vernacular of Queenslanders

to a tang of words – *frangipani, hibiscus, bougainvillea*.
The sky is new rose-gold, as on the first day of the world, I imagine;
hope does not seem out of place.

Ian Potter Centre

Starlings disregard human edifices,
swooping through restaurants and galleries,
for them, all air performance-space,
this cobweb of steel girders and glass

a cubic invitation to flight.
Below, rowing sculls and river boats
slice the Yarra into strips of tea-brown water silk,
which shimmer in the spring wind.

Children ride scooters by the south bank boatsheds.
Crowds line St Kilda Road wrapped in maroon and gold,
black and white, waiting for heroes.
It's a ticker-tape frenzy out there;

one-eyed, my mother would have called them,
and it's become a national trait.
I sip my latte and watch the starlings,
without a need for gods and idols,

although soon I will climb the stairs and weep
before Charles Blackman's *Barbara and Auguste*.
Are they tears for those children across the river,
thrusting into uncertain futures?

We withdraw; they hurry forward.
Arthur Boyd paints *Melbourne Burning*;
already there's concern for tomorrow's final
when a hundred thousand will fan their team's fire;

an oval heart to draw the ire of any arrow.
When I step outside, the barriers are being torn down
and stacked on bleeping trucks
ready for the next emergency.

Lucia

Lucia is a light physicist;
she tells me about photons,
how they can be two things at once,
the way she is Russian and Australian.
She tells me about them again and again.
It's as if she misses them,
her Russian photons,
and can't seem to find them here
at the bottom of the world.
Here, she is a typist,
a slow typist.
She says she's distracted by light
reflected on the keyboard,
and the light-emitting diatoms
of the screen.
I tell her she's the fastest-typing light physicist
in the country, possibly the world.
She smiles: and I notice
the light-gathering quality of a human face;
her smiling face is something
a light physicist could study
for eternity.

Ice sculptor

Waist up, waist down,
two beings frozen into one transparent love.

You feel for this ice maiden and her mate,
know the mark of chisel, and chainsaw,

the places where too much was taken away
or where rough edges stayed.

Through gaps at breast and thigh, light shines,
the rest diffuse – a blurring of the past.

Still, it is something out of nothing,
or nearly nothing, a making out of need half-known.

It is body down to bare bones
and only thirty per cent more water than your own.

The sun does its slow midwinter work;
their kiss melts, smoothing out to loss.

What I would like is this acceptance of the end,
the going down.

If you were the stonecutter in the fairy story you would ache
to be the sun, whose rays hold sway over your creation.

You would go full circle through lust, power, humility
and back to where you are what you can be,

cut out for this art.
And the light will shine through your work

and people will breathe onto it their cloudy breath
as if breathing life into these lovers.

Tribute to Compay Segundo

You roll another cigar,
the phallic enterprise of your days.
Nights are another story:
women clamp the end of your cigar
between their teeth without even asking.
They will hear you from the grave,
plucking that seventh string you added
to construct the music of your homeland.
After twenty years you were still in love
with your lover – a duo made in Havana;
you'd lived long enough
to be back in fashion
and pave the way to salsa.
You're like Beethoven,
a twig between your teeth,
testing the skin of the world,
its soundboard of earth,
island harmonies vibrating your skull,
your last tunes still moving the bones
of feet around the globe.
You worked notes the way you worked tobacco,
a layered arrangement enfolding pleasure,
something to be savoured, loved.
Perhaps Freud did say, *Sometimes a cigar
is just a cigar*, but not in Havana.
And now, I'm listening to your lover –
she's still singing,
and probably about you.

Indian wedding

It's the season for Indian weddings;
gold prices have taken a hike.
If you're into investment, now's the time;
investing in marriage risk of a different kind.
They say the first is a triumph
of imagination over intelligence,
the second, of hope over experience.
That need to belong in another's life makes one thing clear:
we have never learned to be in our own room alone.
I imagine the coiling of hair,

hands and feet red-hennaed;
the groom searching for hours to find his name.
I see silks, silver and gold. I'm told
there are sweetmeats, marquees,
surely a magic carpet or two
to whisk the lovers on a dream journey.
My stars this week foretell marriage,
or else a long relationship is on the cards.
(Though on Wednesday I'm advised to stay home.)
I paste the prediction in my notebook,

alongside shards of poems. I know,
too much Mills and Boon in the formative years.
But when I revisit my childhood library,
its shelves hold no romance.
It's a plain building, next to the war memorial,
the only gold a tribute to our dead.
With gentle fingers we seek names

among the love-script.
Main Street looks the same:
girls still saunter, vain,

all pierced navels and perfect skin.
They don't know the trouble they're in.
I'd like to attend an Indian wedding
when I'm old, then trek in the Himalayas.
Up there, they bury their dead in the sky,
so high the vultures must breathe shallow
as they peck and peck down to bone.
For now, we're giving love another chance,
a second bite of the cherry.
Sixty-five per cent will fail.

Maths used to be my best subject:
logarithms, calculus, algebra.
Faintly I recall the law of diminishing returns.
But I seem to have lost count
or forgotten what I'm reckoning.
Perhaps it's whether, after all this division,
there can still be a quotient of happiness.
Meanwhile, I wear my mother's wedding ring,
its circle of gold worn fifty years thin;
I could pull a wedding sari through its centre.

Rainbow angle

Night writing

First I peel away my skin, dry it in the sun,
take up a sharp instrument, say, a compass,
to needlepoint this ragged page.
I begin writing backwards,
in Louis Braille's six-dot code,
letter by careful letter,
our private words –
the ones I miss hearing –
in an apt, awkward script.
It is *painstaking*, this work,
shifting the pain from where it sits immobile,
in my chest, my gut,
fashioning it into a thing decipherable,
our text written on my body.
Some things need to be spelled out.
To read, you reverse the skin,
run your fingers across it in the dark,
eyes closed, attentive,
the way you touched my thighs
and the forthright code of my nipples.
If you hold this parchment to the light
you'll see bright particles in the dark,
as through an urchin's test, Aristotle's Lantern,
an arrangement of stars.
For a time we were a firmament,
universe-in-a-bed. Now
at night I write letters to you
in this complicated script.
I explain all the things I think are good,

ask the questions I'm not brave enough to ask.
I will send this parchment to you, soon,
for what good is my skin
without your hands?

Myrtle Gully

Up behind Old Farm, mountain takes over.
Myrtle Creek croons to itself in treble and bass.
Each of its tree ferns parades
a crown of new fronds thrust up into green air,
their tips closed tight upon life.
                              Such fists
pummel inside my chest until we climb beneath the waterfall:
ions wash us clean and we align with the rock.
A moss-cushioned log conducts the fall's vibration
through its crumbled heart to our hands;
when you place your fingers on mine,
they, too, tremble.
                    Intricate patterns of fern frond
crisscross above our heads, a lacy wedding canopy,
or, anyway, a delicate shelter for confessions,
a chapel of light, air, water, earth.
            Someone has placed two apricot roses on the pool's surface;
they float, close together, right way up,
among swirls and eddies. We plan our own rite,
a beginning vigorous as the furled crosiers around us.
                                    I reach to uncurl a russet fist;
phallus and vulva, we say, hard thrust and soft welcome,
each tendril a foetus, a coiled promise.
        A sudden wind gusts down the gully,
flustering ferns, a running ripple like an animal's pelt stroked,
or a whisper.
              We stand listening
and count the nine notes of a shrike thrush,
repeated, repeated, unanswered,
each final upward trill a beat of hope.

Body language

Night falls like a diamond-studded silk shawl
about our shoulders,

beginning pale blue, dyeing indigo, then black:
winter has its compensations.

We walk in the light of old stars
feeling brand spanking new,

cruciform bodies at first separate,
like trees, talking through the ground,

then leaning in supple curves
to enfold; we dance our meanings like bees.

Love is a physical thing after all,
made by hand, thigh, breast,

by mind, still flesh; a body language.
And night's a fine thing for lovers,

intimate as the womb.
In your pleasure room we are artisans

of an insomniac craft.
The Kama Shastra tells us there's a science

of erotica and women
take up with elephant drivers for less.

Candour intrigues me, and its lack.
As far back as I remember secrets

got in the road.
But we love to give ourselves away

in the moment.
Outside, the air is cracking with cold.

Laundry hung on the line
will be shot through with icicles.

We savour each other's warmth
and wait for frost to form before we part.

The colour purple

The woman is dyeing her sundress purple.
She has filled a plastic bowl with water,
emptied in a sack of salt.
The packet states the cloth's weight is crucial
but at this point in her life
she has no means of weighing things up.
She's never done this before,
believing all alchemy beyond her.
But the dye's straightforward:
cold-water, aniline.

As she stirs, she imagines dyers
waist-deep in their vats,
the stink downwind of old cities.
If they made the wrong shade of purple
they would lose their heads.
She wonders if she'll smell salty,
like their purple-yielding shellfish.

Afterwards, purple stains will remain on her skin
like blackberry juice, or love bites.

The man thinks the woman's dyeing
means something. He has a clear idea
what he'd like it to mean.
Later he will initiate things,
lifting the hem
and planting his tongue on her purple parts.

Her garden is also making purple,
as if trying to tell her.
Rosemary, sage and forget-me-nots shout;
a lone flag iris grows tight-lipped.
When tulips are out,
she always makes for the black prince,
the night shade.

To her it's the colour of sacrament;
he sees a red rag, a green light,
construes the hue's audacity.
She knows colour isn't even really there:
everything depends on your looking
and in what light you see things.

Just a phase

There's a full moon on my horizon
and planets are lining up a treat;

my feet of clay grow lighter every morning.
Yes, we are our bodies and our geographies,

counting out from toes to tools,
building mind from body.

Our love-making lingers in imagination;
mirror neurons fire:

your hands become my hands,
my mouth your mouth.

When we look away to the sky
and watch the full moon, you say,

It's just a phase.
In childhood I'd wake in the middle of an autumn night:

my father's friend was pruning fruit trees
the lunar way. I got a fright to see

his silhouette against the sky;
now it's your shape I'm learning in the dark.

I sometimes mourn ideas superseded by science:
love is one. Somewhere a statistician

constructs a mathematical model of love,
measuring potential, predicting outcomes.

And there are three theories on why the moon
looms large on our horizon.

When I try to explain them,
you say to turn around and bend over,

place the moon between my legs,
come down to earth.

Hey moon, send down some tranquillity items
to place beneath our pillows:

happiness takes practice
and I'd like to begin.

Milagros

If wishes were fishes, we'd all cast nets into the sea.

Your house is full of charms:
ears and arms, heart and lung,
a jumbled alphabet spelling out desire.
They are amulets worn in secret, or boldly hung
on hems of skirts and slender wrists.
Trinket or talisman cut from copper and tin,
wishes forged within.

Hope is everywhere: see the twists
of paper prayers about a temple tree,
coins aglint in fountains.
We dance three times round a mountain
wishing well, and cast a spell to water sprites.

I will go home and beat silver earrings
with a delicate hammer,
cut the shapes of freedom and heart
from fear and need.
I will wear them on my sleeve.

Be careful what you wish for, I've been told.
Star light, star bright, first star I see tonight …
Have you noticed the stars lately,
the way they're shards of looking-glass?

The truth is, I still believe in miracles:
I wish to be the crab with his hard shell,
slough the old,
live between two worlds;
have fishes' easy habitation of the deep realm;
the turtle's long life;
the owl's wisdom.

The island

We sleep hard up against the cemetery,
walk to the old quartz quarry
gathering pine cones for fires.
The ferry is our clock;
its arrivals and departures
lace stays of the island tight.
We are locked down each night
by Channel dark.

On the crossing we saw light sink
down to big-eyed fish
strung among bones
of whale and whaler.
Now the strait is an iron bar,
today's sky bruise-purple and stark.
Wind roars out the old names:
Lunawanna, Alonnah,
Killora, Mangana.

We tread with care round hollows
that would twist an ankle,
depressions in the forgiving soil
where others have decamped.
There are telltale signs of fires
which once warmed hands and charred flesh.
We sift ashes for fragments,
construct a history.

The stone itself is hollowed,
worn by families returning with the seasons,
enduring, they thought,
before thieves depleted the sea
and laid dignity down under gunwales.

Listen: the wind croons their stories.
Elsewhere, islanders give a whale's tooth
to people they have wronged,
something strong, long-lived and tangible,
something to hold on to.

Rainbow angle

We are standing close enough to kiss,
but don't: this is the wrong end of things.

In our early days, an old man stopped
to watch us kissing;

he waved his walking-stick in the air
and cried *Viva l'amore!*

There was no light between us then;
we were fused at the hip, or the lip,

like the cockscomb oyster: the join
between the two valves stronger than shell.

You said, famously, relationships in this century
will be judged on the quality of endings.

Perhaps that's why we're trying so hard.
We've already had the last supper,

only our leave is left to take.
There is rain in the air

and the sun is low:
I picture a rainbow as background,

bestowing beauty,
perhaps a rare double –

one bow clear, one pale,
colours reversing, distorting mirrors of themselves.

You will recite your mnemonic,
and I mine; we will argue,

playfully, about which is the beginning
and which the end. This is it then,

the never-meeting of minds. A foot apart
we each see a different rainbow;

its centre is found
by discovering our shadows.

We were never as constant as the rainbow angle.
Here is the geometry of seeing:

you and me
and a marvel of broken light.

Honesty

Honesty boxes edge the roadside
all the way down the Channel,
selling raspberries, apples, vegetables, flowers;
here people expect goodness.
It's no surprise to find we live
far from what makes us happiest.
Halfway there we start to sing.

From the deck, we watch sky
move through many guises,
shape-shifting from endless blue
to hues we make up names for.
Clouds leak varga all along Laballardiere,
smudged purple, watercoloured.
At the far end of the beach two boys
are growing away from their beginnings
while the mothers dream.
A scalloped hem of pulling tide
foams between breasts of sand.
Even at this distance, abalone shells
gleam like small sunlit moons.

Later, Cape Bruny's lighthouse blinks at us
its automated blaze. We'd like to signal back
that we are not our ordinary selves here.
We are laughing and drinking wine;
we are being honest.

The boys in their bright flannelette pyjamas
are as beautiful as ripe raspberries;
they are playing with an old pack of cards
but making up a new game,
all their own.

A dream

I was writing a story about patience;
that's what set it off.
About a boy who,
having plucked apples too green,
tries desperately to stick them back on the tree.
I dream of lying quietly in a field of crimson clover
while night falls, and stars fall too,
and the star chart turns above my head,
something I've wished for, the seeing
beyond this human scale which traps us.
I'm waiting, but then I'm not.
And so, too, the boy.
He sees the birds come and go,
the clouds make and unmake themselves,
the stars come out.
He learns some names for things.
And when the apples are finally ripe,
he shares them with his mother,
who is lying in a field of clover,
waiting patiently.

Emergency

PURGATORY

My heroines die at forty-seven
so it's no surprise
I've spent the year on tenterhooks,
afraid to fly, or step outside my magic circle.
But people mostly die at home:
that's where the heart is, and the rest.
In this fleshy apparatus called body
things go awry,
and there are no shopper dockets
for a cheap complete service.
It's a small town; I know the ambo
who arrives at dawn.
He holds my hand as stars fade into morning.
I get a shiny-armoured knight,
white steed stained with a red cross.
In Emergency they work close to a line
usually crossed only once.
This VFL grand final weekend
it's brimful of bashings, cuts and crashes.
At first I can't persuade the gatekeepers
to let me pass. They need death's door
open a crack more. Finally
I slide inside a mighty chamber,
thinking of particle accelerators
and cathedrals,
so while I'm there I pray for more time.
Instead I get morphine
and rise to the top of the list;
somewhere scalpels are sharpened.

Hell

The surgeon's skills are sure-fire
and the registrar's so good-looking
they sedate me. I know the theatre nurse;
we used to drink champagne on Saturdays.
Young then, we'd never had a mortal thought.
This is a little fault from before birth,
tick-tocking, door-knocking.
One more day, they say,
and it would be goodnight nurse.
Ends might not meet; there's talk of bags
and I know they don't mean accessories.
I've always loved punctuation;
talk of colons sets me off.
Can I manage with a semi-colon?
To take my mind off things
I think of words to rhyme with anaesthesia –
synaesthesia, amnesia,
what doesn't kill you, frees you.
Goodnight nurse, I say to her
for a lark as I go under.
I wake up in the art school.
Why is my bed in the drawing department
and where are my charcoals,
the thin willow ones?
There's something I need to express.
Where are you taking me?
Didn't you like my portfolio?
All night terrorists roam the building
in secret training camps while all is quiet.
They project their movies on the back of my blue curtains
so I have to read the subtitles backwards.

I can.
Then it's time for karaoke
and I know the words before they're played.
Visitors won't stop talking war,
while I'm dying for peace.
When I say please move me anywhere else,
nurses get shirty. *Goodnight nurse!*
The morning brings Mrs Mental Health.
Do you know who I am? she asks.
And where you are?
In what sense? I say.
She says, spell 'world' backwards,
count forward in nines,
draw the swastika in reverse.
I ask, *Do you know who you are?*
Whispers wheedle in the corridor;
there are plots against me:
the intern tries to amputate my left arm;
my roommate's son decides to rob my house
while I'm away.
For the first time, I'm scared:
so this is what it's like to lose your mind,
left behind like belongings in another ward.
Next day the curtains quiet down.
They're showing silent movies now
and running fractal test patterns.
I'm looking forward to their plain blue,
the hue they were when I arrived.

PARADISE

In Greek, *eskhara*,
perhaps the name of a craggy isle
topped by white-washed houses.
Like Latin, it puts a good spin on things.
This one a scar-let: thin, and vivid red,
tracing the dark *linea nigra*
once plumb line to my pubis.
Two scars meet up, intersect,
seven years' neglect wearing the last one silver.
A T-junction on my belly then,
a place to stop and decide on east or west;
the test will be in years to come.
It's hard to make a poem
out of minor disembowelment:
no ritual, no dignity;
it's plain old blood and gore,
like movies you see in commercial cinemas.
A young intern says the operation was exciting,
and successful, as if she were a spy behind enemy lines.
You should have been there, she quips.
Last time, I tell her, *I was*. A needle in my spine,
a newborn tucked under my chin.
But since my cells replace themselves in seven years,
was it even my same skin?
Back then I heard a surgeon read the future in my entrails.
I've used up one chance; I'm down to the guts of things,
down to knowing how thin that line.
I am emergent, like consciousness,
a possibility where there was none.
That was almost my life.

Things to do around Hobart

Drive to the brand new sea wall;
sit on a shiny bench and breathe salt air.
This is especially good after two weeks in hospital
looking at blue curtains.
Borrow someone's dog
and walk the length of Bellerive beach
watching the light on the mountain
and the way spinnakers billow.
Play giant chess with your son at Salamanca.
Walk from the Mt Wellington Springs to Sphinx Rock,
up Lower Sawmill, along below the Organ Pipes,
and climb the Zigzag track.
December is best, when the waratahs
push up their petal candelabras
and you can dip your tongue for nectar.
Ask someone at the pinnacle, nicely, for a lift down.
Lie on the university lawns
and look up through the trees.
This also works well at the Botanical Gardens.
Wait in silence to see a platypus,
or two, at the Hobart Rivulet. Jump
with children into Brown's Rivulet
and ride its current out to sea.
Remember to laugh and squeal a lot.
Ignore health warnings: it's worth the risk.
Listen to the whole dawn chorus in South Hobart
while lying in your lover's arms.
Applaud at the end; thank the paprika bird
and the one which sounds like a happy man

out for a Sunday stroll.
Be that man: stroll everywhere.
Go to the fish punts and buy fresh trevally;
bake it whole for someone you love.
Sit and watch the fishing boats bob
before you go. Drink wine on the pier
with one of your friends, or seven.
Lie under your lover's olive tree
and watch the light for hours.
Plant an olive tree yourself.
And a lemon. And a lime.
There will be more good times.
Be ready.

I want to be a cow
(*After Selima Hill*)

I want to be a cow
and not my child's keeper.
I want to be a cow;
I am already ruminant,
chewing the cud of years,
rendering them digestible,
swallowed lightly, absorbed.
I want my four stomachs to do their work quietly.
Grass is not the diet people aspire to –
routine and stringy.
Hay adds variety and bulk;
clover has even the most sedate
kicking up heels and head-tossing
as if the wildness was back in their bones.
But you can have too much of a good thing.
Mostly, cows are not flighty like that,
nothing like horses.
They are calm in the traces, steady, even dull.
They do whatever it takes.
I want to be a cow and not miss that appendix,
that cecum. It's not that there's anything
wrong with methane;
that depends, like most things,
on how it's used.
Truth comes out in the end.
I want to be a cow
expecting nothing but the known.
I want healthy haunches for the bull's cover,

a full udder, someone calling me home
morning and evening.
There is some envy:
the neat attire of belted galloways,
formally turned out, looking
coiffed and cared for always,
even when they're not;
the crump-backed brahmin's
loopy ears and dowager's hump,
endurance without hunger, without thirst;
the brangus' night-time disappearance.
I want to be a clever cow,
happy in my own skin and paddock,
a cow that accepts boundaries
without a zapping shock, over and over;
a cow that realises grass is not greener
on the far side of the fence.
Clever enough, too, to know a bolt to the brain
is always at the end of this story,
and despite Temple Grandin's distant, kind designs,
there may be fear; that's up to me.
I will practise calm and prepare well.
It's the calves you fear for,
not the self; that sweet young flesh, that gallivant,
that highfalutin show of heels.
They live as if there's no barbed wire,
no bolt, only life.
I want to be a cow
and take one blade from their paddock,
the green, delicious, precious blade.
Let's face it, we're all domesticated,
our ancient untamed lives

a moment's dream.
You lose track of offspring,
confuse their smells.
Some end up overseas.
Don't kid yourself,
they don't come back.
None of us makes old bones.
That's okay: I want to be a cow,
but not an old cow.
I will not suffer aged indignities
like those of the hospital ward.
If the prime of life is all I get,
I'm content. Watch me graze,
gaze, dream. Watch me simply stand.

The dark zone

The dark zone

Sassafras Creek burbles along its course,
scrapping with sticks and stones,
eddying about the ankles of children.
We set up camp on its bank,
breaking five tent pegs in the pitch;
summer earth won't forgive.
My son plucks up courage
and joins some boys' ball game,
aware of the shape our family isn't.

Then you arrive in your hatchback
and unfold like a circus,
squeezing into the last site
right beside us: three children,
tent, stove, camping table-and-chairs.
You set up your big top in the dark;
voices and laughter close by are a comfort.

Sassafras Creek keeps me awake all night,
till my skull is a cave,
made by running, dripping water.
Are we having fun yet? I ask my son.
He says, *Got to have vitamin F.*

Rugged up for the constant below-ground temperature,
our families meet outside Marakoopa Cave.
Soon, your tears tell the story of a loved husband
some years dead, how every anniversary
you place a wreath at those traffic lights,

and wonder if the truck driver
also remembers, also returns.
You say, *It makes me sad to go camping.*
But I promised myself I'd take the children.

We have entered karst country,
hollowed beneath us
like the skulls of seals,
all sinus crevice and scrape;
it is a honeycomb of cavities.
If we walk out into the bush
our feet will stumble in saucer-shaped dolines,
sweet-sounding depressions of collapsed limestone.
Sinkholes disguise themselves as lakes.
The ground we tread is far from solid.

Speleothems: formations of calcite,
but the word sounds like champagne flutes.
Beside stalactites and stalagmites,
helictites grow sideways, twisting;
there are shawls and flowstones:
it is impossible to know
how anything will turn out.
We practise old mnemonics about ceiling
and ground, hear new ones
to do with tights falling down.
My son wants to take the lead from our guide,
and enter each cavern first.
Only when she turns off lights
and we experience pure darkness
does he change his mind.
We can't see a hand in front of our face;
it's like not existing.

Glow worms glow, as they do, in their dark.
We learn about cave spiders
below the spark of their stomachs,
how creatures adapt to a lack of light.
It is not necessary to have eyes at all
if everything is dark, so the eyes have gone.
If there were light, I would glance across at you.

I ask if the caverns have romantic names
like those I remember from Japan –
ceiling of an umbrella shop,
den of the dragon's teeth –
but, no, science prevails.
There *were* such names,
but everyone's forgotten.
A single drop of water falls as we watch,
scattering minute particles of calcite.
Time is visible – this moment
the beginning of aeons.

Thoreau said a lake is the eye of the earth;
this cave is the ear
with its long canal and cavities,
its coiling intricacy.
It has heard another tale of grief,
carried it away into the dark zone.

Emergence into light is hard
now we know the marvel of this hidden realm.
My friend has held a key to the cave for months,
like a sorceress; she knows
this entering, this leaving.
It's rebirth, she tells me,

from the womb of earth.
The thing is, that's how it feels.

If super-colliders are the new cathedrals,
I'd rather worship in these catacombs,
sacrificing anything I can think of,
with the certain knowledge that Earth
has formed us, and made us who we are;
it is earth we'll become.

The next time we meet – in a theatre –
it is also dark. You are playing cello.
When the lights come up
you smile straight at me.

Elegy for the loss of laughter
For Anne

My friend is smiling in the newspaper
because she must. She tells me
inside her smile is upside down.
She ends her emails with a down-mouthed smiley.
Rilke claimed that happiness is mere moments

stolen from loss,
happiness and loss sides of a coin.
Take a girl's happy wave goodbye
as she steps up to her life,
not knowing the rest of her life is missing.

My friend will watch her daughter wave goodbye
for the rest of her days.
The Chinese have a saying:
When the heart weeps for what it has lost,
the spirit laughs for what it has found.

What have you found, my friend?
If you could fathom complex calligraphy,
would you find laughter?
Or have you only noticed suffering everywhere?
Did you know that in a day

children laugh forty times more than adults?
I notice the words *daughter*
and *laughter*. One letter changed,
a shift of vowel, a single fricative, a schwa.
I think of words which rhyme with each:

daughter with *water* – essence of life,
laughter with *after*, forever after.
I've made her laugh myself,
wanting to leaven the black bread of grief.
My friend has a secret:

butterflies hold her daughter's laughter;
they crowd around her with silent messages.
She wears them made from silver or glass,
pinned or clasped close to her skin
so they can't fly away.

A sci-fi film invents our world without children:
schools have closed, there is no need of them.
Laughter will die out too,
till no one even remembers it.
There were butterflies that day at Bolton's Beach

when she sat with us, our legs in a rock pool.
We laughed each time a tiny creature
ventured, nervous, from below the rock shelf.
Our reflections rippled over the surface,
fragmenting, until there was no image.

Once, people told their grief to the bees,
who flew them away and turned them to honey.
What would we tell them?
That a girl stepped into her life,
laughing.

The heart is in the room

VIRTUAL REALITY
Today I try a heart transplant myself.
The steps are simplified,
and minus the blood.
Scream down through the sternum
with the Stryker saw;
prop the split sides apart;
transfer your patient to a heart-lung machine;
open up the fibrous glove pericardium;
cut away the front of the old heart
leaving the back to receive the new;
replace it with the healthy heart;
connect up all the pipes;
put everything back the way it was.
Bind up the sternum with wire, which will remain,
like a spiral-bound notebook that contains notes on surgery
and is hell at airports.

THE HEART IS IN THE ROOM
The courier deposits an Esky on the theatre floor,
rushed from one hospital to another,
from van to plane to van,
tragedy to hope.
The heart is in the room, the courier cries.
Surgeons and nurses spin to stare;
the fresh heart is there,
cooled, alive, resting,
the old heart already gone,

its job now done by a mechanised heart and lung.
Connected, this new heart will start by itself,
the patient's nervous system remembering its work,
blood rushing through the heart like a river.

MEMORY OF CELLS

What might this heart remember?
Strange change can overcome recipients;
ten per cent experience the donor's presence.
One patient develops a passion for extreme sports –
couch potato to tri-athlete in months.
Another begins writing love poetry.
Yet another makes up with estranged siblings,
does work for charity, and is kinder to his wife
than since their courting days.
He quips, *I've had a change of heart.*
Why wouldn't memory reside in the heart?
We are fish without scales;
fish learn with the whole nervous system,
respond with their bodies to danger or food.
We respond with our bodies,
but forget to notice. Once,
warriors ate the heart of an enemy
for his courage.

SPARE PARTS

It's not only organs in demand –
bones, skin, tendons, arteries, joints:
a set of leg bones fetches twenty thousand dollars,
corneas sixty thousand, tendons a thousand apiece.

Soon we'll grow our own spare parts,
stem cells directed to become anything.
In a transplant operation on television
a courier arrives with a fresh young liver
to replace one sclerotic.
Doctors tidy up the healthy liver,
hold it high to admire.
Beautiful! they sigh.
Surgeons have sewn two donor arms
onto a man born armless, till now unable to hug.
And the first face-transplant patient wakes up,
someone else staring in the mirror.

Equations of motion

There is a man on the bridge tonight,
at its highest point,
as if the words *apex, pinnacle, apogee*
have private meaning.
Perhaps it comes down to equations of motion
and he knows something I don't.
His arms are slung over the rail
the way he'd dally at a neighbour's gate;
he's outside the bars.
A policeman and policewoman
try their best to persuade him
hold on.
As I drive past I wonder what they say;
all three appear calm.
His face is that of anyone you know
and he is dressed in jeans and shirt;
he might be going to the movies.
I don't see if he's wearing shoes;
I'm told they're mostly removed
and placed neatly together, pointing out.
Police cars block the nearest lane
and traffic backs up into Rosny.
Four lines of cars continue past,
realisation dawning on drivers
that this is no accident. The radio advises
a detour via Bowen Bridge.
I want to wind my window down and shout
Don't do it! People have *died* off this bridge!
I'm accelerating away from him,

a bottle of wine and video
on the seat beside me;
I have plans for tonight.
But now I'm recalling: velocity
is displacement divided by time.

Five monks at Woolies

Three Tibetan monks in grey robes
sit on the supermarket entrance bench.
All appear to be at prayer.
The youngest has only her fingertips together,
delicately, as if what they touch is fragile.

Next to her, an older monk's hands
form prayer position, palms joined.
The next has her hands in her lap.
Two more monks stand inside the supermarket,
facing the car park.

All have their eyes closed.
I study faces and physiques:
their shaven heads and uniform grey
make it hard to say who is man or woman.
Has prayer time caught them on the hop,

and they've dropped everything to pray,
trapped behind sheet glass?
Perhaps they're giving thanks
for this neatly shelved bounty,
a kind of grace.

As one, they end their stillness
and begin to make hand signs to each other
regarding the five trolleys loaded
with bulging plastic bags.
Perhaps these monks don't speak

and there is silent order to their lives.
I know their home,
two streets from mine.
It used to have a swing set and tree house.
The monks cut down the trees,

making it more like their homeland.
They removed the swing set.
They have a big truck to travel in
and need to park it in the yard.
I've read there's one small monk among them,

a boy named Buddhaholy, whose visa has expired.
Everyone is fighting to keep him here, safe.
On the anniversary of deadly demonstrations,
the Chinese close Tibet. The boy
dreams of a tree to climb, a swing set.

Secret war

Children dig with sticks in the ground,
keen as beavers: there's good money to make.
But all the bombs will never be found.
They risk lives for the family's sake.

Keen as beavers, with money to make.
Twenty US dollars for a whole bomb casing.
Children risk all for their family's sake.
At five, or six, too old for childish games – marbles, chasings.

Twenty US dollars for whole bomb cases,
or they're used as superior village-house stilts.
No thought of childish games on these young-old faces.
Nothing is done to assuage forty years' guilt.

Bomb casings make sturdy foundation stilts
where all else is bamboo or thatch, flimsy, handmade.
Why is nothing done to atone for the guilt
of no-place-to-hide from two hundred and fifty thousand B52
    raids?

Here, all is flimsy and handmade,
unlike sleek machined bomblets, their payload of bearings.
There was no shelter from nine years of daily raids.
Who comes to find how the victims are faring?

One hundred bombs per plane, packed with bombies, packed
    with bearings;
they are scattered in forest mulch like exotic fruit.
This is how the survivors are faring:
they lose lives, lose limbs; they are still being hurt.

A bombie lies among leaves, an exotic fruit.
The little girl understands its worth.
She's heard she could die, lose her legs or arms, get her friends
    hurt.
Still she squats, weighs up. Is it the truth?

The girl is hungry; she understands its worth:
money for a month without hunger.
Squatting, thinking, weighing things up. Who has ever told
    the truth?
But her village is full of half-arms, peg-legs. This is the shape
    of danger.

Death is hard for her to imagine; so is a month without hunger.
Bombs are forbidden fruit, buried treasure.
Experts arrive, tell her this is the shape of danger.
As they ghost it away under sandbags, her sense of loss is hard
    to measure:

'*All that metal!*' Here, bombs are forbidden fruit, buried
    treasure;
they feature in every picture schoolchildren draw.
Their sense of loss at safe disposal knows no measure;
they secretly hope for more fruit from the secret war.

Bombs appear in pictures the children draw,
like treasure maps of the Ho Chi Minh trail.
Children secretly hope for more fruit from the secret war;
and hope the disposals will fail.

Disposal officers have treasure maps of the Ho Chi Minh trail
but all the bombs will never be found.
Children secretly hope the disposals will fail.
They dig with sticks in Laos ground.

Brancusi's kiss

I see it through a Dublin store window.
Ignorant of art and icons,
I imagine some ancient Celtic carving
dug from an outer island,
its scale huge, a megalith.
When I describe the sculpture
friends produce a name: *Brancusi*.
Later, in Japan, at Hakone Open-Air Museum
I find Brancusis on the lawn,
but never the kiss I'm after.

Here it is again, black and white;
a single block, it sits in his studio
among myriad geometrics and abstracts.
Two faces, bodies, squashed together,
eye-to-eye, mouth-to-mouth, embracing,
arms strong along the sides;
the lovers have never let go.

I learn it was carved as a tombstone sculpture,
a kiss to last a loved one for eternity.
There is no light between these lovers;
the carve lines minimal; it is almost an ashlar –
one square-cut chunk of stone for building;
I imagine it used by mistake,
the builder's surprise finding lovers in his wall.
I imagine many copies constructing a kissing wall,
where lovers come from round the world
to kiss instead of pray,
prayer in its own way.

At seven, Brancusi worked as a shepherd
in the Carpathian mountains.
He taught himself to carve wood,
whittling away long days
spent with his sheep and sheepdog.

Here, in the Man Ray photograph,
two dogs are fervent disciples
hungry with love for him,
claiming his lap, his clothes,
as if they still smell sheep.

Brancusi walked from Romania to Munich
to Paris to reinvent himself.
At art school, he stuck messages on the stairwell walls:
Remember you are an artist! Don't be discouraged!

Brancusi is his own work of art:
peasant-artist.
He lived in his studio
and cooked for guests in his kiln.
They sit among these sculptures
at 8 impasse Ronsin,
The Kiss right there, centre-stage.
I think a kiss like this prefers privacy.
His guests eat, taking covert glances.
They go home and make love,
reminded they're not kissing enough;
they've forgotten its importance.
Watch teenagers, Italians:
they'll sit like this, locked together.
Scientists give many explanations for kissing;

Brancusi knew more:
death,
life.

Oracle bone script

(On Jao Tsung-i's exhibition:
The Amalgamation of Mind and Universe)

This is the oldest script,
more hieroglyph or rune
than the complex ideograph of later dates.
It is copied from the telling cracks
in ox bones and tortoise shell.

Holes were drilled with stones,
bones heated over fire
to craze in ways the diviner understood,
each splintering line interpreted, copied down.
It is a script constructed

from an age-old desire to know the future.
We could have inherited a tea-leaf kana
or the cursive of a gutted newborn goat.
Who knows how these things begin, or don't;
only the marks are passed on.

These are Jao Tsung-i's delight:
his metre-long bamboo brush extends his arm,
his sight, each sign distinct,
a challenge to his overflowing ink,
separate like drum beats, bell tolls,

only meanings brim into someone's fortune.
This is a long sentence,
marching down rice paper on its silk scroll,
rolled into recorded history.
There is no translation;

perhaps no one's left who knows the runes.
Their shape is the thing,
each as beautiful as a flower.
Elsewhere the master creates his own blooms:
he uses the brush of blond bamboo,

crooked as an old man's back.
Straight arm, crooked brush:
like a koan.
Again the brush is long,
perspective gained with distance.

He paints the traditional four old gentlemen:
orchid, bamboo, plum blossom, chrysanthemum.
And here, across four scrolls, is the lotus,
its long stem his great challenge;
it must be a single stroke,

no sign of hesitation, of doubt.
Later, at ninety-two,
an old gentleman himself,
he has a waver in his brushstrokes,
in his paintings of west by east.

But what does Jao Tsung-i care?
He has discovered the secret of life
and painted it down:
half a cup of red wine;
an elegant zither across my bed.

Spyhopping

Hand-finned and singing sensation around the globe,
you are your own salt separation factory,
constantly homesick and probably pregnant.
Grey nomad of the deep, you travel north each year,

gliding among sea mounts and upwellings,
living off muscle and blubber.
You're a bulky beast, a moveable feast,
spyhopping along the coast, spotting familiar landmarks

the way kids do on roads home.
Perhaps you have a magnetic map and a head for directions;
you may use the sun and the stars,
or follow songlines of ancestors.

What's with all this song-singing and pelagic palaver anyway?
You've long been queen of the sea shanty:
do you realise you've gone platinum here on the risen seafloor?
Whatever it is you say to people, it seems to calm them down

so let's blast the humpback song from airships over Syria.
At our favourite pub you're etched in leadlight,
the Derwent aquamarine, then scarlet;
sails of barques billow beyond longboat harpoons.

It's said that women in dainty lace-up boots
stepped, blue back to blue back,
across the river without a toe getting wet.
That's a whale of a story, when women wore about their bodies

parts of whales, in corset stays, push-up brassieres and perfume.
Parasols boasted baleen ribs. Men sought ambergris
(those vomited blobs of squid beak) to ease nights, please wives.
And still a thousand whales a year are killed, flayed and flensed.

(Have you heard the one about the man who swallowed a whale?)
They say they want your earplugs to measure rings of growth,
find out how old you are. Not as old as you would have been.
Alive, you're still good for business: whale-watching cruises

and *Save The Whales* T-shirts instead of scrimshaw.
Why don't we let you be? Why don't we save us all?
My son stomps on Salamanca's trypots,
calls them witches' cauldrons; he drums up

a few spells to bring back the whales.
I tell him that this year numbers are up:
eight thousand six hundred whales traffic our eastern seaboard,
seen among them one white male like Ahab's.

Perhaps it was he who smooched a Sydney-to-Hobart yacht,
mistaking the racing hull for a pale, svelte mate,
snapping its keel, the crew left all at sea.
What can be said about your love life (other than it's big)?

Some males try being gentle, and persuade with a long and tender
penis. Others are rough and biting, or gang up.
Afterwards those love rudders fold away as neatly as ironing boards
and just as hard, testes tucked up by the stove of other organs.

You've got to keep your powder dry, and warm.
And have your wits about you in the shallows:
eighty cousins strand at Marion Bay, death writ large on sand.
Beached whales, I called us in antenatal class,

pods of bellies aground on littorals of change.
For nine months our young swam internal seas,
transiting the fish stage, trying out gills,
abandoning tails in favour of legs,

re-enacting our exit from water.
A humpback whale foetus bears the marks of its past –
throwback hind limbs, vestiges of teeth beneath baleen:
none of us are beyond change.

If we played the fossil record on a phonograph
(itself endangered) we would hear the strains of evolution.
Your name is a parsing of the past:
animalia chordata vertebrata mammalia

cetacea mysticeti *balaenopteridae*
megaptera novaeangliae;
a prayer said in Latin
that you survive.

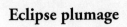

Eclipse plumage

The fencer and his mate

His chainsaw wakes us every morning – reveille: the first post –
it bites into quiet and birdsong. The fencer's back,
his wild vibrating instrument in a maestro's hands; he cut the iron-
bark himself in the next valley; now he saws it to the heart,
x-ray vision finding six fenceposts inside each log the way Michelangelo saw
his prisoners. Also freed is a totem pole of red and resin. The sculptor

wants to fly the heartwood home, show it at a European gallery with other sculptures
in a hemisphere where ironbark is exotic. Found art. He wonders could he post
it, or take it on the plane. He has seen the necessary cut away; once back
he will teach others to look differently at what remains. The fencer's iron
crowbar bangs each strainer into its final resting place, his heart
also under strain. His shouts are loud, rhythmic, like those of ardent lovemaking, the saw

and its easy mechanical art now abandoned alongside his blue wheelbarrow. I also saw
his blue camping chair and blue Esky arranged like a still life, a sculpture,

like large scale trinkets in the satin bowerbird's bower. This is the post
from which he surveys his craft: he sits and runs his eye along the lines, turns his back
then spins as if to catch the fence out. His strength is honed to iron
but the lines and patterns of this work he knows by heart;

it's work he's taken on since his father died on the Diamond Rio. It's the heart
of the matter, because of when he was a lad and what he saw.
The big truck gleams blue and silver down in the bush and its sculpted
chrome is polished with love. A loose post
caused his father's fall between truck and load, breaking his back.
The fencer has no need of pencilled marks on the iron-

bark: the pattern is carried in his head like the spider with its web, like his iron
determination to buy back the truck, to go on working in this heart-
land of his childhood, of his father's. The lyrebird's taken up the fencer's grunt, the noisy saw,
and will continue for weeks after this fence is finished. The bird sculpts
sound with his show-off syrinx and his dance upon a hidden lookout post
on the ridge. Visitors will wonder if the fencer's back

again. His job is done, surely. But he will always be back
for others. Ten years he gives the fence: the wood's like iron
but the six wire-strand holes he drills through each post's heart
are a help to grassfires, and can let the barbed wire rust like a saw
left out in rain. He'll return, in his short shorts and singlet, sculpted
muscles rippling and sliding under blue-tattooed skin as he hefts each post

in place. Among the tattoos is a fencepost; serpent and love vine entwine it on shaved skull, his back.
People fear the iron in the fencer, and his tattoos, but there is also a big heart
just below his shoulder blade. I saw it. I saw his fence. I saw his sculpture.

Ironbark shavings curl on red earth like scented locks of Pre-Raphaelite hair; straight
wires through each fencepost a hexagram of pride. At twelve dollars a metre enough now earned
for a good weekend. The fencer and his mate escape to a woodchop carnival. An axe
to them is aesthetic in the extreme. They feel its weight in their palms like a woman's breast: true
they might call it, or keen. Their own axe never out of sight. *He even sleeps
with his*, says the fencer. *It's only new,*

95

says the mate, *and I keep the cover on.* I've heard he's new
but a natural, six wins under his belt since Christmas, a stroke so straight
and sure it takes away the crowd's breath. It's quick this sport, like a very fast orgasm, earned
by readiness, as well as work. And there's no denying the pleasure: swing of the axe,
roar of the crowd, atmosphere, booze. They joke about drug tests. And is it true
about the women? *It's hard on the missus,* they say. Wives sleep

alone at home when the men travel; they are woodchop widows. *We don't sleep
around, but,* the fencer says. They shake their heads, the idea of new
loves slowly circling. *Got to keep your strength up, stay straight,*
says the mate. They're serious, these two. I've seen the fencer down tools for a hard-earned
break and, instead of sitting on the blue chair, uncover his axe
and split a log in seconds. What they say about axe blows *ringing* is true.

Out over the Shoalhaven and up to the ridge each true
blow rings like a birdcall, one among many, and the lyrebird learns it in his sleep.
Like the bird, these men are alert to making new
their repertoire. They take up the double saw, recognising trust between them, straight
talk and determination, the pairing of bodies. They've already earned
a reputation on the carnival circuit. The double saw has nothing on the axe,

no beauty; it's harder to love. The partner replaces the axe
in this double act; it's the person you put your faith in, prime. *True
blue*, they would say. And they enact these movements in their sleep:
the look, the simultaneous start, the give and take, something new
learned between them at each comp. Three and a half hours' drive to Sydney straight,
chop all day, then turn around and drive home, talk all the way. The prize earned

is nothing to the sense of satisfaction, elation; they show no emotion though it's earned.
No show ponies here, says their coach. It's like a good axe to an axe-
man, a feeling to be weighed, enjoyed in private, something true,
like finishing a fence. It's technique, not strength; even little blokes can do it. Sleep
might bring dreams of fortune, fame; top axemen earn half a million a year. A new
ute is all they'd like, to bring down their practice logs to the troughs, to keep them straight

and moist and ready. To tell it straight, what they earn
is each other's love, that feeling like an axe, something fine and true,
like a sound sleep, two lives made new.

Eclipse plumage

I read in my bird book of females'
changed feathers after breeding:
eclipse plumage.
They become undistinguished.
Here, my colour has come back.
It's all the walking, I say.
The fresh air. The land.
Silly, I know, but I grin
all the way to the river.

Paddock bull

This brangus bull can hold a pose
better than an artist's model
or a yogi.
He has his cud to chew,
and all four stomachs may be growling,
but he shows no agitation.
Even cows lowing in the next paddock
don't distract him
though I detect a little bit of pink interest,
his blackness otherwise unbroken
but for the dash of yellow plastic in one ear.
He's a paddock bull, I'm told:
this boy never gets the girl,
never proved himself,
just hangs around looking beautiful.
Hopeless, the manager tells me.
It's all arranged husbanding here.
Now he bides his time
watching active bulls come and go,
calves get born,
seasons change,
watching strange creatures like me
admire him.

Woman with yellow flowers

The light will not stay still for the *plein-air* painter;
its swift track across river flats
deposits darkness in every crevice
and has her rushing inside for purple.
Time travels too fast, then too slow.
At dusk she returns with an armful of yellow,
wattle blossom from the riverbank;
she had waited for the sun to leave with its load of bees.
In her studio, she ignites a canvas.
She can't know that one Saturday soon
her own landscape will ignite,
engulfing everything with a terrible energy:
this is how innocence looks.
The next day, wind roars down this valley like an ocean
and the water pump cuts in and out with a sob.
A bird rackets, exploding the bamboo thicket,
with that unmistakeable sound of the need to escape.

Bundanon

I've woken too late for kangaroos:
they'll be lazing down in some hollow by the river,
grazing on sunshine made yellow by wattle.
Bees will lull them into reverie.

It's Saturday; it's quiet: the artists are sleeping late.
Outside my window, crimson rosellas step in and out of shade,
highlighting the brilliant register of their feathers.
Currawongs brabble in the grass.
Later I will find a single feather of brilliant green
and bring it home.

What do we make our memories from
if not these small things?

By six, night will fill this valley like a river,
black brangus cattle the first to disappear,
drowned in darkness.
The painters will come inside and wash their brushes.
All day they've been looking;
now they want to know what it is they've seen.

A rose is a very different thing at noon than at midnight,
and the bush here will also change its chemistry in the dark,
breathing differently, like a lover dreaming of the loved one.
Wherever we look for bio-chemistry we will find it
and you must admit mathematics is also there,

but I am seeking something else:
memories out of air,
moments from ink.

The bend in the river

I like it when we near the fenceline
where riverlight meets sky
and a sharpening of the eye for detail
takes place. Today, a divot of red earth
where an eastern grey has leapt the fence
while his mob squeezed through below;
fresh excavations by wombat-in-the-road;
a fistful of scarlet-tipped feathers.
You are better at detail,
seeing shadow patterns and glancing light.
I notice, but don't know what to make of things.
From our nest in the soft grass
we spy on a settled, roosting bird;
I guess *kingfisher*.
You explain the plumping-up of feathers
can make species hard to identify.
I hardly know myself here;
I am someone from my past,
someone at ease, someone laughing,
someone with all the time in the world.
It's a heady combination.
When the bird leaves,
its flight pattern gives it away.

Diamond python

Spring's offerings:
flame trees on fire, wattles abuzz with bees,
new brangus calves in the home paddock.
Once I see a fox slink
from the bush boundary
and trot across the land as if born to it,
a reminder that things are never right
in paradise. Boyd's lovers were expelled;
they knew all along it would happen.
Expect the payola, they'd whisper
at they trysted.
We lie on a ridge-top boulder;
beneath us the diamond python wakes
from his winter sleep, hungry for summer;
his tongue smells lust above his lair.
Could you allow yourself, you ask, *to fall asleep here?*
Later we will crisscross the river plain
looking for the grave of the drowned horse,
which tangled in barbed wire.
We expect to find an X-marked spot,
but there is often nothing to show for tragedy.
We walk on, to the riverbank
and consider taking off our clothes.
It's too early really.
Instead we skim stones
and watch for an hour
a white-bellied sea eagle watching us.
One day we do fall asleep,
curled like kittens in sylvan sunshine

after picnicking in the black wattle bower.
There's nothing to be done;
we've said the timing isn't right,
but all day we will wonder,
What if it is?

Lovers below Brasso tin
(After a 1962–63 drypoint by Arthur Boyd)

They lie, these lovers,
in a field of white.
It may be pure, but that's unlikely;
no, they are trying to break open the light

and see beyond the spectrum,
like insects, fish.
Infrared and ultraviolet
are said to symbolise truth and fiction;

both are beyond where we set our sights.
On the page, these lovers are suspended in lust:
limbs entwine like the monkey rope vine
on the spotted gum, sinuous and tight;

they are climbing clockwise to dizzy heights.
There is ambivalence in the limbs,
while their minds are suffused with frenzy.
Fantasy and a labyrinth of thoughts enmesh;

it will be hard to find their way back
without a very long string of words.
Perhaps they have been inflamed by the blatant coral tree:
its cadmium red and layered labia

are hard to ignore, like the eroticism of ideas.
The brain, remember, is the largest erogenous zone,
no matter how sensitive one's earlobes, or toes.
The bed load here is not the Shoalhaven's pebbles and stones

but a river of past lovers, hopes, vulnerabilities.
It is hard to predict the pattern of sediment
or when things might settle.
They may end up giving birth to constellations;

this is one act of love in an endless passion play.
Next time, they will lie side by side,
not touching, and each will tease with a story.
She will talk of elephants' feet

which contain rare cells more sensitive than the clitoris;
he will tell her which colour he sees when he comes;
their artist knew there was cruelty in sex.
They are caught between what they have

and what they want;
add fear, shame, desire, guilt,
and you understand restraint
in drypoint black-and-white.

Men without sorrows

You are the one who taught me to see:
you gave birds like a gift, one of many.
You found them in paddocks,
among coral trees, on the riverbank,
up on the ridge where we slept on the rock
as if lovers.
Galahs: *ga*lah, you called them,
as if they were festivals
of pink and grey.
The grey goshawk's single-minded
hover and prey
beside the glide of pelicans
is a perfect demonstration:
two kinds of wing,
two kinds of flight.

You have taken some birds with you –
crimson rosella, satin bowerbird, white-bellied sea eagle –
you are looking into them for truth.

So much is closed to us, off-limits,
beyond the knowing we can know:
why it might be wrong to love someone.

We admire Brett Whiteley's birds,
how bold they are, how true,
portraits and self-portraits.
You are smitten with his paint;
you want to eat it.

You smuggle birds out of the country
disguised as colour;
among their covert feathers
are secret meanings,
codes only we can crack.
I like the way you tip a canvas
and let paint flow,
guided only by the impulse
for down, down.

The birds here are bright
as if there never were predators
and they could parade with equanimity.
I imagine old rainforests,
flowers equally brilliant.
Some birds' colour comes
from a scattering of light particles
through the structure of feather barbules,
their hooks and curls shattering the spectrum,
the satin bowerbird's blue, say,
which we notice in the sunshine
just before he sings his falling fireworks;
some colours birds need to eat.
We joke: *Eat your greens!*
Earn your stripes!

Is the yellow sucked from wattle
and the urine of brangus cattle?
Orange from the pineapple fruit,
red from the coral trees' claw-like blooms,
purple from the climbing love vine
which winds itself around me?

A willy-wagtail skips into view
and waggles his tail so joyfully
we fall down laughing
and can't get up.
Instead, we lie there
watching clouds stream overhead.

There's a critical period for birdsong,
as there is for language
or for animals finding their way in the world.
Kittens raised without horizontals
fall down steps.
Is there a time when the heart is sensitive,
the mind clear,
when love must be learned,
or never can be?

What else must be learned?
Ways of saying *I love you* without words,
ways of wishing you well when you are gone.
Sometimes love is like that:
not possible, or allowed.

I'm that hungry boy beneath a tree of green apples
knowing all he has to do is wait
and time changes everything.
So impatient.

I want to fly north for winter,
sun on your shores.
Like the South African swallow
I would learn local tunes at each rest stop,
rehearse them on the wing
to sing when I reach you.

It's called *instinct*,
but birdsong extends beyond call or care,
beyond necessity. Is it practical,
theatrical, an axis of joy?
Who can say it's not for the sake of beauty?
We consider that question,
hoping to learn of our own purpose.
What's your instinct? you ask.

Let's say we have an instinct
for knowing where we are in the world,
and who makes the best mate.
Let's say language and mathematics,
aeronautical science and painting are instincts.
It doesn't get us far.

Flight is more accessible than song,
a matter of muscle and mind,
physics, those phenomenal feathers.
Still astonishing.

On the last day, a necklace of white ibis
appears and disappears against the blue sky,
like a wedding gift
given and taken away.

All morning the birds string themselves out
as if skywriting goodbye.
From my bus, I see that flock
in a paddock, down to earth,
like dancers who've removed fine costumes,
pretending they know nothing of aerial beauty.
I feel like them, going home.

There, time flies by, without birds' wings,
more like small angels
in a hell of a hurry. They whip up
a flurry of air as they pass;
it can feel like a brush against my skin,
a caress.

I sleep warm under down,
collect nests and feathers,
watch a pair of superb blue wrens
court, mate and build a nest in my garden's jasmine.
Wrens never learn:
they always build in the way of danger.
There are disappointments:
stillbirths, early deaths,
betrayals.
I've read that if all falls apart early in the season
they start over,
take another stab at love.

It's hard to remember to wish for the possible.
Instead, I wish for wings.
I would spread my wings with certain purpose
and sure-fire knowledge of my course,

navigating with everything to hand –
dead reckoning, landmarks, magnetism, visual flow.
I'd migrate with the wintered birds,
follow your early departure,
escape this tight bodice of human-ness,
learn to soar.

There's an old Arabic saying: men are birds without wings
and birds are men without sorrows.
Birds seem to have the best of it.
Despite all appearances
the world is discontinuous,
split into separate parts;
we are two.

Contentment

We are not good at knowing what makes us happy;
sometimes all it takes is a walk over flood plains,

rich in kikuyu grass and the sour smell of marsupials.
The play of sunlight on a river might do it, if it's wide

and calm and edged with white sand.
Or chitter of parrots on the wing.

It's important to forget minutes and hours,
to measure time in sandstone and shadow.

Pebbles of contentment will collect,
form a sediment and grow deep,

a foundation for days.
This landscape's motifs are the thermal winding

and unwinding of a pelican's glide,
eastern grey kangaroos' arcing dominion,

wombats. Each day I expect them at intervals,
time my own diurnal wanderings by appearance

and disappearance. Today you walk with me
to watch the pelican's flight;

we sing him into a holding pattern,
notes rising to settle among axillaries, coverts.

Wing prints weave plaits of air above us
as we track flight paths of crimson rosellas,

currawongs, galahs.
We practise their dialects – whistle, ululate, hoot –

enacting origins of language,
if not with these sounds, then with eyes, bodies,

hands that signal intent.
I invent notation for these birdcalls:

an impossible task,
like trying to pin down right and wrong.

I've fallen in love with the names of your paints –
phthalo blue, ultramarine, umber –

and the night sky you make from them,
pierced by a paper moon and stars.

It's not that there are more stars,
but that we can see them together.

I tell you Mars is approaching –
the bathers by the river saw it,

the astronomer saw it; everything will change.
You say, *We all need something to look forward to.*

Across the Shoalhaven, a dead tree is chain-sawed for firewood,
next winter's warmth to be stored,

as comforting in its woodpile pattern
as the promise of love.

Meanwhile the crow despairs, the kookaburra laughs,
and I'm wondering what they would name our cries

in the night. Are they joy, or pain, or both, inseparable,
paints already mixed on a glass palette?

Holy days

New Year's Eve
(After 'Fireflies' by Fred Chappell)

We leave our patch, clamber through a fallen barbed fence,
disintegrating any border.
The night has darkened, become immense
and warm; the western sky is out of order,
afire with crazed horizontal lightning
bolts, sheets of sheer light, and thunder
crashing about our heads. Otherwise frightening,
tonight all is adventure; I am under
your wing; we sing in our safe harbour,
and seem to call up a moon so huge and silver it makes no sense.

As if from a moonless planet, we stand and stare
at its monstrous birth: this lit sphere
rising out of science into myth as it rears
itself from earth, into the deranged, black, ten-to-midnight air.

One summer

In the summer of our content
we are putting ourselves back into our bodies,
fogging our minds with heat.
We stand on your Juliet balcony naked,
the touch of air like that of kisses.
Or was that you, behind me,
your thighs gleaming tree boughs?
Below us, the olive tree's leaves
are gleaming in moonlight,
like the welcome lights of a town
after a long time at sea.

Measure

Your long-legged stride marks out Connelly's Beach.
This familiar strip of sand
stretches more than a kilometre and a half.
You start him, he sprints;
you time him, he records.
Sometimes I race him, or you do.
All this for my son.

Our footprints have appeared and disappeared
on this beach countless times,
formed, washed away,
a palimpsest of large and small, of varied journeys,
impressions of us painted by landscape.
I have walked alone, or with others:
they say adults have seventeen close friends;
most of mine have walked here beside me
even those from far away.
I bring them to where I'm most myself.

It's where we made love one New Year's Eve
under a big black sky,
wind whipping up a frenzy of waves,
drums and guitars still playing round the campfire
and fireworks still falling in our mind's eye.

Today we have the whole white crescent to ourselves;
the bay is calm, smooth as milk,
under a clear blue sky;
you can't help but think of phrases
like *heaven on earth*.

My son is obsessed with running fast and measuring:
How fast, Mum? How far? How long will it take?
We take our time.

Later we sift deep shell drifts for maireeners,
the kind we've seen in shell necklaces like Truganini's,
still made by local elders,
strung with patience, knowledge, love.
I show my son how they shine beneath a dull exterior;
sometimes you have to know exactly *how*
to discover beauty.
It will take weeks, months, years to collect
for a bracelet, never mind a necklace,
but he starts a jar now,
full of expectation.

I used to make shell necklaces on Hawley Beach,
my mother saying fairies made the shell holes
to help little children do just that.
I tell my son sea urchins
drill a hole to get at food inside.
Truth is also extraordinary.

At one end of the beach a pair of pied oyster-catchers
wades in limpid shallows;
at the other end, a pair of sooty oyster-catchers
does the same.
They act as guardian lions,
this beach an entrance to their sea
like the fine gravel before a Buddhist temple,
the crunch of footsteps across it
transition from profane to sacred.

Life's beach is long, serene and beautiful,
or windswept, storm-wrecked.

A shell drift gleams bright white near the creek
where you scattered your wife's ashes
before I knew you.
I often brought my son there to play,
as every boy needs a creek.
There are other things a boy needs:
someone to start him off,
to yell encouragement,
to praise, record, celebrate.

The olive tree

I put *The Cloudspotter's Guide* away
and gaze into such a dense Cycladic blue
it's hard to grasp the notion
that the sky starts here.

I am in the sky; the olive tree is in it.
Yet I see the tree against the blue,
leaves turned every which way –
white, grey, shades of green.

The olives have ripened
by some alchemy of winter sunlight
and air sharp with mountain snow.
They hang like the soft eggs of a night swallow –
black, and nearer by, purple,
some glinting like Lucknow mirror-work,
a silver-backed fragment finely stitched to each.
I pluck one; roll its mammalian warmth in my palm.
I press out juice – crimson, blood-like,
as if I've cut my thumb
in some blood brother tryst.

Underneath this tree I've been dreaming
of France's Mediterranean coast;
nearby a spotted turtle-dove coos:
Pourquoi pas? Pourquoi pas?
It is time for moving on.

In the afternoon, we pick a bucketful of olives,
my son up among the silver branches.
France could be like this, I say,
a warm harvest, a bounty.
I feel like the teenaged Colette,
poor, but cellar-rich.
I'll practise phrases: *joie de vivre*,
printemps, *amour*;
I'll pack all the clichés in my suitcase
and when Customs ask if I've anything to declare,
I'll say, *You bet!*

I think of the botanist so enamoured
of leaves' fight for sunlight, for life,
that he develops a flying bicycle
and glides above the tree canopy
of the Amazon forest, astonished.
If he flew above this olive tree
what would he see?
Glittering leaves and a woman
stretched beneath them, dreaming,
her face tilted towards the sun,
inside her sky.

Shy

So shy, platypus of the bedroom;
it comes in only at night,
wraps itself around my waist and thighs,
strokes my breast and buttocks,
nuzzles, sometimes settles on my belly.
Gone is the begetting,
the wearing, the faring well.
Here in the dark,
all is fine.
I recognise this creature,
but even with a mirror
it would not know itself.
What am I? it might ask,
and worry, like the bunyip
in the picture book.
Do not name it;
do not try to catch it.
It will hurry to its long burrow
and won't be seen for days.
Unnamed, it stays to play
and play a game as old as us.
Names are not everything.
I can love a tree for its bark
and spread, the leaf shape,
the way it turns in light from green to silver,
in autumn from red to yellow
and still not know its genus.
I can lean against its strong trunk
and breathe in what it breathes out.

I can love the way it stands so still,
alone, and is satisfied.
It is what it is, despite me.
That bunyip knows what he is
only when he meets another.
But that's a children's story.
In the adult world
we like to know what's what;
Psyche couldn't save herself from looking.
Can I?

Piano

You open the lid of polished wood
tenderly, as if a coffin for viewing,
unlatch and lift away the front panel,
exposing vulnerable innards.
You show my son how it works,

your long fingers stroking keys,
gentle hammerings of wood and felt
on taut wires – muted, extended, stopped.
You've stored your saddest things
in this shiny cabinet of sound;

now you take some out and play them.
I once saw a pianist dive inside his grand piano
and pluck its strings, any intercession
between mind and music of a sudden unbearable.
We say *heartstrings*.

A seahorse lies on the shore of our cortex:
hippocampus – the visceral brain.
Here, pyramid cells line up side by side,
orderly, despite chaos in the world perceived.
A psychologist once dubbed it the emotional keyboard.

This is the instrument you play,
or it plays itself, like a pianola,
you pedalling your pain,
the music sliding down your arms to us.
It's as if you've unlatched your skull

and let me see how you work.
Music is our mother tongue:
heartbeat, breath, running feet,
the soft percussion of rain,
flugelhorn wind.

Oh, I breathe, and my heart beats;
I sob and wail and laugh.
But now I think,
plangent, melancholic, woebegone,
wanting words to surround

and bring things home.
And who wouldn't love music's words?
minim, crotchet, quaver,
arpeggio, glissando, tremolo
But I don't understand its mathematical meticulousness

and precise patterns,
barely distinguish flats from sharps,
one octave from another.
In your courtyard I watch olive leaves dance with sunlight
as the wind strums innuendo.

We listen to music with our muscles, wrote Nietzsche,
and now my muscles are getting tight.
I am wondering about your silent music,
all the rests together,
the something not expressed.

A professional musician once explained
the value of accidentals,
the way they change everything,
and double sharps which move you forward.
It's my one regret.

You could, I suppose, at this late date
teach me piano.
Or you could gather me in your arms,
tenuto; I am a note
waiting to be held.

Night

The night sky arrives fast. The moon
cradles its shadow side in its silver saucer.
The milky way shines ghostly white,
and all the constellations
in this galaxy's central plain
become a breathtaking bright.
The biggest stars, or closest, ripple
silver lines across the black bay.
One falls, brief and burning, like a love affair, a life.
We eat tinned soup, and flathead we've caught;
we drink all the wine. Along Quarantine Bay,
other yachts raft up and light masthead lamps.
Children's fluting voices carry clear across the water.
We make love below sea level
and sleep in the warm womb of boat, cabin,
the bay so calm our bed is as still as a house.
A few inches away octopus, skate and tiny fish
nibble at the hull we painted deep blue in summer.
I like that there is no room for us
to move away from each other.

Holy days

I.

On the first day we find a coconut
washed ashore; you break it open on a log;
we drink its milk and eat the rough white flesh.
I think *communion*.
We eat – fish and bread and wine –
by the beach, below coconut palms
under a bright moon.
Each night we walk along the sand,
you tilting towards the sea, me towards you.
There are always, and only, two sun beds
left somewhere along the shore.
We lie on them and watch the night sky,
eat ice cream, and kiss like teenagers.
A fruit bat skims between palms
like a momentary dark thought from the past
and then is gone. A stone curlew
steps up to us, this slip of a dinosaur,
and does its blood curdling.
We watch planes come blinking in
from north and east. Planes are formal:
they punctuate a holiday like this,
capital and full-stop to a carefree line;
I try not to think about them.
We take a forbidden late-night dip in the pool,
make love with no need of covers.
We sleep wound up in each other's body.
We get up late and feast on tropical fruit;
we go naked inside, or wear sarongs.
Who are these people?

II.

In our garden there are hibiscus,
palms taller than the buildings
and plants with fronds like parasols.
In the rainforest we see a rare gardenia
and cycads which survived the last ice age.
It's hard to take in when all you've seen
for years has been familiar.
This is like a life-and-death task in a legend:
Make the most of every moment!
Or a holiday novena,
each day a bead from a rosary decade,
something to hold in your hand, caress, meditate on.
In the middle of the third day
I join the weeping paperbarks
and can only think it's because I'm happy.
These gentle giants lean into the steady tropical breeze,
shedding reams of red bark
as if they, too, want to be naked.
I tear away a thick strip
on which to write this future poem.

III.

At the gorge, we walk beyond tourists,
off into the rainforest
then along the coursing riverbed,
climbing boulders, crossing rapids.
You always want to look around the next corner,
sail beyond the next headland,
but I swear you must have known all along
that clear round jungle pool.

My oldest friend says, *Things fall into place*,
but, really, you don't expect it.
Two brilliant blue Ulysses butterflies
skitter and flap above the pool, then alight on a boulder.
They quiver there together – wings up, wings down –
as if signalling. I know what they say.
The river roars among the granite boulders
which are taller than a man, pale stone elephants;
they have come a long way over millennia,
thundering down from Manjal Dimbi and the tableland,
and are as smooth-worn as skin.
The pool-bed is ground from them,
gleaming white gravel becoming sand.
We weigh up smooth stones in our palm,
as if hunter-gatherers off to stun an orange-footed scrubfowl
fossicking on the forest floor.
Your stripling body is bright in the water;
you look pleased with yourself.
I, well, I am beyond-the-pale *ecstatic*,
a sinner beatified by light and baptised.
There is danger: the placid pool's deep fast water
would suck you down between sunken rocks
and, like a demon lover, keep you there
until you began to love it.
Amethystine pythons unwind in the trees.

IV.

You take me to a beach you discovered while I slept,
praising its long sand-shadows when the sun sinks
beyond a fringe of mango trees,
its view to Double Island.

We lie in the shade of a thatched bush,
like an ancient desiccated mangrove,
a multi-planed hedron,
whose poppy-like apricot blooms open as we watch,
then fall to the sand
in a quick, beautiful, life-and-death flowering,
their part in all this done;
they are as delicate as tissue paper,
as petals pressed inside a poetry book,
with bright yellow stamens and black centres.
We have no names for things here
so look more closely.
Patterned spiral shells I've never seen
still house life. At home,
I'll discover they're called sundials,
or architect shells.
We find cowries, white-lipped.
Only later do we see that sunbathers here are naked.
Some are brown all over; others have white hips,
breasts or chests. White feet.

v.

On Green Island the instructor tells us,
Hold hands! What could be more romantic?
We've tried, our hands almost coupling,
but haven't got the knack underwater:
flippers scoot us off in different directions,
our masks fill up with water,
sometimes it's hard to breathe.
After a time, we feel more like our ancient selves,
at home in sea water, calmly finning above the reef.

Many creatures inhabit this between-world,
water and air, air and water;
we become them –
seals, cormorants, dolphins.
Below me, grazing on seagrass,
is a young green turtle,
young, yes, but also aeons old,
more ancient than I can grasp.
This would be a terrible time to drown,
but excitement almost does me in.
I grab for your hand, your hip, your ankle.
You have to see this!
Our eyes keep meeting through our masks
all the way back to shore;
we'd grin but for the snorkels.
Okay, we didn't manage the hands
but in this mute world
you swimming beside me is enough.
Later at the night markets you buy me a red sarong
printed with turtles
and I wear it in our kitchen as we cook.

VI.

On the last night we wait on the beach
for the moon to come up
but have mistimed. We've eaten all the prawns
and drunk all the champagne
before it lifts itself out of the cloud bank.
Yes, it's an *indulgence*.
As a child, and in my church,
this word meant punishment was cancelled,

everything forgiven.
They've skipped purgatory
and sent me straight to heaven.
Yes, the stone curlews are still raucous
and an occasional fruit bat swinging by overhead
makes us flinch.
Nothing is *perfect*,
but here we are, breathing.

Skin

Given that the average adult man's skin
covers 1.9 square metres,
the average woman's 1.6,
we have a big, private pleasure garden
where we might rest, or play,
or while away a whole day.

Fingers, toes, hair, tongue can run loose.
And like a garden for the blind, it's full of scents.
We love to walk the coast, forest,
mountain, rivulet, but we can stay home,
and explore this intimate 3.5 square metres
with equal fascination: it's a private sanctuary,

a national park for two.
When we met, your skin sent out defences
to do overtime on replacing cells,
creating a layer of protection.
You were afraid I would get under your skin.
Marvel that cells assemble at all,

let alone as flesh and bone,
as fingers which stroke a thigh, or a breast.
In cross-section, our skin is an aquarium,
crammed with exotic fronds and stands of seaweed.
No wonder we get that underwater feeling.
Here, a wreath of flashing nerves espaliered along limbs,

a jungle of blood vessels,
a tree canopy of corpuscles.
And here are tiny muscles which pull the hairs up straight
when you're cold, or afraid, or aroused.
Here are the pores of sweat glands.
When the last sweat is secreted after lovemaking,

and the skin grows super-sensitive,
these glands will settle down a while.
We are like slow comets
leaving a trail of skin cells,
a path to follow home,
eighteen kilos shed in a lifetime.

We've already lost a lot
and want to make the most of what is left.
The whole epidermis is already dead;
the rest will follow suit:
now is the best place
for everything.

Acknowledgements

Poems in this collection have appeared in *Island*, *Australian Book Review*, *The Australian Literary Review*, *Famous Reporter*, and the following anthologies: *The Best Australian Poems 2007*, *The Best Australian Poetry 2008*, *The Newcastle Poetry Prize Anthology – to sculpt the moment*, and the *Henry Kendall Award Anthology 2010*.

I am indebted to Arts Tasmania and the Australia Council Literature Board for grants to work on this collection. I would like to thank Felicity Plunkett for her support. Thanks also to Adrienne Eberhard for our conversations.